Over-the-Counter Derivatives Markets and the Commodity Exchange Act

Report of
The President's Working Group on Financial Markets

November 1999

November 9, 1999

The Honorable J. Dennis Hastert
Speaker of the House
United States House of Representatives
Washington, D.C. 20515

Dear Mr. Speaker:

We are pleased to transmit the report of the President's Working Group on Financial Markets entitled <u>Over-the-Counter Derivatives Markets and the Commodity Exchange Act</u>.

One of the most dramatic changes in the world of finance during the past fifteen years has been the extraordinary development of the markets for financial derivatives. Over-the-counter derivatives have transformed the world of finance, increasing the range of financial products available to corporations and investors and fostering more precise ways of understanding, quantifying, and managing risk. These important markets are large and growing rapidly. At the end of 1998, the estimated notional value of OTC derivative contracts was $80 trillion, according to the Bank for International Settlements. In addition, these global markets have been marked by innovation in products and trading and settlement mechanisms.

A cloud of legal uncertainty has hung over the OTC derivatives markets in the United States in recent years, which, if not addressed, could discourage innovation and growth of these important markets and damage U.S. leadership in these arenas by driving transactions off-shore. Recognizing the important role that derivatives play in our financial markets, and the dangers of continued legal uncertainty, the Working Group has spent the past six months focusing on OTC derivatives and examining the existing regulatory framework, recent innovations, and the potential for future development. At the request of Congress and the Chairmen of the Senate and House Agriculture Committees, we have prepared the attached report, which reflects the consensus we have reached on a set of unanimous recommendations.

The Working Group is recommending changes to the Commodity Exchange Act ("CEA") designed to:

- promote innovation, competition, efficiency, liquidity, and transparency in OTC derivatives markets, by providing legal certainty for OTC derivatives and removing impediments to innovation (specifically to the development of electronic trading systems);

- reduce systemic risk, by removing legal obstacles to the development of appropriately regulated clearing systems;

- protect retail customers from unfair practices, by providing the CFTC authority to address problems associated with foreign currency "bucket shops"; and

- maintain U.S. leadership in these rapidly developing markets through a combination of the measures outlined above.

We, the members of the Working Group, therefore respectfully urge the Congress to give serious consideration to our proposals to help achieve these goals.

The Federal Deposit Insurance Corporation, the Federal Reserve Bank of New York, the Office of the Comptroller of the Currency, and the Office of Thrift Supervision reviewed and commented on this report and support its conclusions and recommendations. We are grateful for their assistance.

We appreciate the opportunity to convey this report to you, and we look forward to continuing to work with the Congress on these important issues.

Sincerely,

Lawrence H. Summers
Secretary
Department of the Treasury

Alan Greenspan
Chairman
Board of Governors of the Federal Reserve System

Arthur Levitt
Chairman
Securities and Exchange Commission

William J. Rainer
Chairman
Commodity Futures Trading Commission

November 9, 1999

The Honorable Al Gore
President of the Senate
United States Senate
Washington, D.C. 20510

Dear Mr. President:

We are pleased to transmit the report of the President's Working Group on Financial Markets entitled <u>Over-the-Counter Derivatives Markets and the Commodity Exchange Act</u>.

One of the most dramatic changes in the world of finance during the past fifteen years has been the extraordinary development of the markets for financial derivatives. Over-the-counter derivatives have transformed the world of finance, increasing the range of financial products available to corporations and investors and fostering more precise ways of understanding, quantifying, and managing risk. These important markets are large and growing rapidly. At the end of 1998, the estimated notional value of OTC derivative contracts was $80 trillion, according to the Bank for International Settlements. In addition, these global markets have been marked by innovation in products and trading and settlement mechanisms.

A cloud of legal uncertainty has hung over the OTC derivatives markets in the United States in recent years, which, if not addressed, could discourage innovation and growth of these important markets and damage U.S. leadership in these arenas by driving transactions off-shore. Recognizing the important role that derivatives play in our financial markets, and the dangers of continued legal uncertainty, the Working Group has spent the past six months focusing on OTC derivatives and examining the existing regulatory framework, recent innovations, and the potential for future development. At the request of Congress and the Chairmen of the Senate and House Agriculture Committees, we have prepared the attached report, which reflects the consensus we have reached on a set of unanimous recommendations.

The Working Group is recommending changes to the Commodity Exchange Act ("CEA") designed to:

- promote innovation, competition, efficiency, liquidity, and transparency in OTC derivatives markets, by providing legal certainty for OTC derivatives and removing impediments to innovation (specifically to the development of electronic trading systems);

- reduce systemic risk, by removing legal obstacles to the development of appropriately regulated clearing systems;

- protect retail customers from unfair practices, by providing the CFTC authority to address problems associated with foreign currency "bucket shops"; and

- maintain U.S. leadership in these rapidly developing markets through a combination of the measures outlined above.

We, the members of the Working Group, therefore respectfully urge the Congress to give serious consideration to our proposals to help achieve these goals.

The Federal Deposit Insurance Corporation, the Federal Reserve Bank of New York, the Office of the Comptroller of the Currency, and the Office of Thrift Supervision reviewed and commented on this report and support its conclusions and recommendations. We are grateful for their assistance.

We appreciate the opportunity to convey this report to you, and we look forward to continuing to work with the Congress on these important issues.

Sincerely,

Lawrence H. Summers
Secretary
Department of the Treasury

Alan Greenspan
Chairman
Board of Governors of the Federal Reserve System

Arthur Levitt
Chairman
Securities and Exchange Commission

William J. Rainer
Chairman
Commodity Futures Trading Commission

TABLE OF CONTENTS

Over-the-Counter Derivatives Markets
and the Commodity Exchange Act

Report of
The President's Working Group on Financial Markets

I.   Introduction

Last year, Congress indicated that the President's Working Group on Financial Markets (the "Working Group")[1] should work to develop policy with respect to over-the-counter ("OTC") derivative instruments,[2] and the Chairmen of the Senate and House Agriculture Committees requested that the Working Group conduct a study of OTC derivatives markets and provide legislative recommendations to Congress.[3] This Working Group report focuses on changes to the Commodity Exchange Act (the "CEA") that are necessary to promote innovation, competition, efficiency, and transparency in OTC derivatives markets, to reduce systemic risk, and to allow the United States to maintain leadership in these rapidly developing markets.

The Working Group has concluded that under many circumstances, the trading of financial derivatives by eligible swap participants[4] should be excluded from the CEA. To do otherwise would perpetuate legal uncertainty or impose unnecessary regulatory burdens and constraints upon the development of these markets in the United States. The Working Group has also concluded that it is important to remove legal impediments to the development of electronic trading systems, which have the potential to increase market liquidity and transparency, and appropriately regulated clearing systems, which can reduce systemic risk by allowing for the

---

[1]   The Working Group is composed of the Secretary of the Treasury, the Chairman of the Board of Governors of the Federal Reserve System (the "Federal Reserve"), the Chairman of the Securities and Exchange Commission (the "SEC"), and the Chairman of the Commodity Futures Trading Commission (the "CFTC").

[2]   H.R. Rep. No. 825, 105th Cong., 2d Sess. 991-92 (1998).

[3]   Letter from the Honorable Richard G. Lugar, Chairman, Senate Committee on Agriculture, Nutrition, and Forestry, and the Honorable Robert Smith, Chairman, House Committee on Agriculture, to the Honorable Robert Rubin, Secretary of the Treasury (Sept. 30, 1998).

[4]   Under the CFTC's current exemption for swap agreements, 15 C.F.R. pt. 35, "eligible swap participants" are defined to include various regulated financial institutions, business enterprises that meet certain tests relating to total assets or net worth, certain pension funds, state and local governments, and certain wealthy individuals.

mutualization of risks among market participants and by facilitating offset and netting of contractual obligations.

Specifically, with respect to OTC derivatives, the Working Group is unanimously recommending:

- An exclusion from the CEA for bilateral transactions between sophisticated counterparties (other than transactions that involve non-financial commodities with finite supplies);

- An exclusion from the CEA for electronic trading systems for derivatives, provided that the systems limit participation to sophisticated counterparties trading for their own accounts and are not used to trade contracts that involve non-financial commodities with finite supplies;

- The elimination of impediments in current law to the clearing of OTC derivatives, together with a requirement that any clearing system for OTC derivatives be regulated by the CFTC, another federal regulator, or a foreign financial regulator that satisfies appropriate standards;

- A clarification of the Treasury Amendment that clears the way for the CFTC to address the problems associated with foreign currency "bucket shops" and excludes all other transactions in Treasury Amendment products from the CEA, unless they are conducted on an organized exchange;

- A modification of the exclusive jurisdiction clause of the CEA to provide greater legal certainty to hybrid instruments; and

- A statutory clarification of the inapplicability of the Shad-Johnson Accord to hybrid instruments that reference securities.

The Working Group understands that the development of OTC derivatives markets also raises questions about the regulatory structures applicable to exchange-traded derivatives and implicates statutes other than the CEA. Accordingly, certain additional issues, including the level and scope of regulation applicable to exchange-traded derivatives and the conditions under which the trading of single-stock futures contracts might be permitted, are also discussed in this report. In deference to the CFTC's views about the need for further Congressional direction with regard to its exemptive authority, the Working Group as a whole believes that the enactment of its recommendations with respect to OTC derivatives should be accompanied by explicit authority for the CFTC to provide appropriate regulatory relief for exchange-traded financial futures if deemed by the CFTC to be consistent with the public interest.[5]

Although this report recommends the enactment of legislation to clearly exclude most OTC financial derivatives transactions from the CEA, this does not mean that transactions may not, in some instances, be subject to a different regulatory regime or that a need for regulation of currently unregulated activities may not arise in the future. Specifically, although the Working Group recommends excluding certain electronic trading systems for OTC derivatives from the CEA, the enactment of a limited regulatory regime aimed at enhancing market transparency and efficiency may become necessary under certain circumstances if, as such systems develop and grow, prices of transactions executed through the systems come to be used widely as the basis for pricing other transactions (i.e., the systems come to serve a price discovery function). If so, depending on the specific market, existing regulation, and the problems that regulation would be meant to address, the CFTC's expertise in exchange-traded derivatives could make it an appropriate choice to serve as regulator. The Working Group members will continue to monitor and consider the desirability of regulatory or legislative action to address issues that may arise in the future.

The Working Group looks forward to working with Congress to develop legislation to implement the recommendations contained in this report.

---

[5]   Such authority should not, however, permit the CFTC to provide exemptive or other regulatory relief from the requirements of the Shad-Johnson Accord. See infra note 16 and accompanying text and infra part VIII.A.

II.   Over-the-Counter Derivative Instruments

The market for OTC derivatives has expanded steadily and rapidly over the past two decades. At year-end 1998, the total estimated notional amount of outstanding OTC derivative contracts was $80 trillion, reflecting an increase of 11 percent from June 1998, according to data from the Bank for International Settlements ("BIS"). In contrast, exchange-traded futures and options contracts amounted to just $13.5 trillion at the end of 1998, down almost 6 percent from the end of June 1998.[6] According to BIS, the vast majority of OTC derivatives are interest rate and foreign exchange contracts (72 percent and 26 percent, respectively); equity-related contracts make up only 2 percent of the market, while tangible commodities account for a fraction of a percent.[7]

Activity in OTC derivatives markets has been primarily concentrated in three types of instruments: swap agreements, options, and hybrid instruments.[8] The typical swap agreement is a contract between two parties providing for the exchange of cash flows based on differences or changes in the value or level of one or more interest rates, currencies, commodities, securities, or other asset categories. These cash flows are calculated with reference to a principal base (known as the "notional amount") of the underlying asset category. Because the notional amount of a swap agreement is only a contractual term used to calculate the amount of payments under the swap agreement, it generally is not exchanged between the parties to the agreement. Accordingly, the notional amount is not a measure of the value or the riskiness of a swap agreement.

An option is an instrument that provides the holder with the right, but not the obligation, to buy (call option) or sell (put option) a specified amount or value of a particular underlying interest at a specified price on, and in some cases before, its specified expiration date. Typically,

---

[6]   Bank for International Settlements, Quarterly Review: International Banking and Financial Market Developments (Aug. 1999).

[7]   Bank for International Settlements, Press Release, The Global OTC Derivatives Market at End-December 1998 (June 2, 1999).

[8]   The terminology used to describe derivative instruments is not precise. Certain complex derivative instruments (for example, "swaptions") combine the characteristics of both typical swaps and options, and the term "swap" is often used to refer collectively to typical swaps, options, and instruments that combine characteristics of both. Similarly, the term "OTC derivative" is usually meant to refer to all of these instruments and sometimes is meant to refer to hybrid instruments as well, although hybrid instruments are frequently listed for trading on securities exchanges and issued in standardized tranches and therefore are often not traded over-the-counter. Unless the context otherwise indicates, the terms used in this report are meant to be construed broadly.

OTC options provide for cash settlement, rather than delivery of the underlying asset, or a choice between the two methods of settlement.

Hybrid instruments are depository instruments (i.e., demand deposits, time deposits, or transaction accounts) or securities (i.e., debt or equity securities) that have one or more components with payment features economically similar to swaps, forwards, options, or futures contracts.

Traditionally, the exchange-traded and OTC derivatives markets have differed in several respects. Exchange-traded instruments — principally futures and options — are standardized as to their material terms and conditions, whereas the terms and conditions of OTC instruments may be negotiable between the parties to the contract and reflect individualized credit decisions. The customization of these transactions to individual customer needs as to maturity, payment intervals, or other terms has allowed customers to adjust individual risk positions with greater precision. Exchange-traded instruments, however, may offer market participants the advantages of liquidity, price transparency, and minimal credit risk. Whereas transactions in the OTC markets are conducted almost entirely between institutions on a principal-to-principal basis, exchange-traded markets are also accessible to retail customers conducting transactions through futures commission merchants ("FCMs").

As OTC markets develop, however, the extent to which market participants engage in large numbers of transactions with similar terms increases, because certain instruments serve the risk-management needs of a large number of market participants. Thus, the opportunity to negotiate the terms and conditions of an instrument may exist, but in practice this opportunity may not be used to a great extent for certain types of instruments, such as certain "plain vanilla" interest rate swaps.[9] Moreover, although the widespread use of innovations such as electronic trading and clearing have the potential to increase efficiency and reduce systemic risk, they could also blur some of the distinctions between exchange-traded and OTC instruments.

---

[9] Nevertheless, counterparties typically have negotiated a "master agreement" that sets forth terms and conditions, including netting and collateral provisions, applicable to all transactions between them.

III.   Legal Certainty (Enforceability of Contracts) and the Development of the CEA

Legal certainty is a crucial consideration when parties to OTC derivative contracts decide with whom and where to conduct their business. Parties must be certain that the contracts into which they enter are permissible in the governing jurisdiction, that their counterparties have the legal capacity to enter into the contracts, and that the provisions of the contracts are enforceable. An environment of legal certainty for OTC derivatives and their execution and clearing will help to reduce systemic risk in the U.S. financial markets and enhance the competitiveness of the U.S. financial sector.

For OTC derivative contracts, uncertainty arises from concerns under current law as to whether some of these contracts could be construed to be subject to the CEA and whether certain types of mechanisms for executing and clearing OTC derivatives might be construed to alter the legal status of otherwise exempted or excluded instruments. These concerns force financial institutions to evaluate legal risks when developing new instruments and new risk-management initiatives and have the potential to reduce the flexibility and competitiveness of U.S. financial markets. In light of the size of OTC derivatives markets and their importance to the U.S. economy, to other markets, and to U.S. financial institutions, these concerns must be addressed.

The CEA subjects contracts for the sale of a commodity for future delivery and options on such contracts to the exclusive jurisdiction of the CFTC.[10] The CFTC also has jurisdiction over commodity option contracts, although the CEA does not unambiguously characterize the CFTC's jurisdiction over such instruments as exclusive.[11] In addition, transactions in, or in connection with, commodity futures contracts and commodity options contracts must be conducted in accordance with the CEA and regulations promulgated by the CFTC. In general, this means that, except as provided by certain administrative exemptions currently granted by the CFTC, transactions must be conducted on, or subject to the rules of, a contract market designated by the CFTC.[12] The CEA defines "commodity" to include specific agricultural commodities and

---

[10]   7 U.S.C. § 2(i). The CEA also provides that the term "future delivery" does not include any sale of any cash commodity for deferred shipment or delivery. 7 U.S.C. § 1a(11).

[11]   7 U.S.C. §§ 2, 6c. But see S. Rep. 93-1131, 93d Cong. 2d Sess., reprinted in 1974 U.S.C.C.A.N. 5843, 5870; International Trading Ltd. v. Bell, 556 S.W.2d 420 (Ark. 1977), cert. denied, 436 U.S. 956 (1978).

[12]   7 U.S.C. § 6(a), 6c.

"all other goods and articles, ... and all services, rights, and interests in which contracts for future delivery are presently or in the future dealt in."[13]

In 1974, Congress amended the CEA to state that "[n]othing in this Act shall be deemed to govern or in any way be applicable to transactions in foreign currency, securities warrants, securities rights, resales of installment loan contracts, repurchase options, government securities, or mortgages and mortgage purchase commitments, unless such transactions involve the sale thereof for future delivery conducted on a board of trade."[14] This statutory exclusion, known as the "Treasury Amendment," was enacted at the request of the Department of the Treasury ("Treasury") as part of the same act that expanded the definition of "commodity" from a list of specific tangible products to the broad definition contained in current law. As discussed in more detail below, however, the exact scope of the exclusion has been the subject of litigation.

Uncertainties concerning the jurisdictions of the CFTC and the SEC to regulate certain securities-based derivative instruments also arose from the amendments to the CEA enacted in 1974, which gave the CFTC exclusive jurisdiction over all futures, whether the underlying instrument was a physical commodity or a financial commodity.[15] The same amendments provided, however, that the jurisdiction of the SEC was not otherwise superseded or limited. These provisions have created conflicts regarding each agency's jurisdiction over novel financial instruments that have elements of securities and futures or commodity options contracts.

In an attempt to clarify the scope of the CEA and to permit the trading of certain stock index futures, the SEC and the CFTC agreed to specify which financial instruments fell within each agency's jurisdiction. This agreement, known as the Shad-Johnson Accord, was codified by Congress in 1982 and 1983 through amendments to the CEA and the federal securities laws.[16] The Shad-Johnson Accord amended the CEA to explicitly prohibit futures contracts based on the value of, or any interest in, an individual security (other than certain "exempt securities"),[17] or a

---

[13]   7 U.S.C. § 1a(3).

[14]   7 U.S.C. § 2(ii).

[15]   7 U.S.C. § 2(i).

[16]   Futures Trading Act of 1982, Pub. L. No. 97-444, 96 Stat. 2294 (1983); Act of Oct. 13, 1982, Pub. L. No. 97-303, 96 Stat. 1409.

[17]   "Exempt securities" include government securities and certain other securities that are exempt from many of the federal securities laws pursuant to Section 3 of the Securities Act of 1933 or Section 3(a)(12) of

securities index that does not satisfy the statute's criteria as to the composition of the index. The Shad-Johnson Accord also gives the SEC authority over options on (i) securities (including exempt securities), (ii) certificates of deposit, (iii) foreign currencies traded on a national securities exchange, and (iv) groups or indices of securities; and gives the CFTC authority over futures contracts and options on futures contracts on (i) exempt securities (other than municipal securities), (ii) certificates of deposit, and (iii) indices of securities that satisfy the statute's criteria.

To address concerns about the legal status and enforceability of OTC derivative contracts, the Futures Trading Practices Act of 1992 (the "FTPA") amended the CEA to provide the CFTC with authority to grant exemptions from the CEA for any transaction or class of transactions that meets certain criteria.[18] The FTPA did not specifically address whether or not any particular type of transaction, such as a swap agreement, is a futures contract or an option. The Conference Report language, in fact, made clear that the CFTC could grant an exemption without finding that the transaction is a futures contract subject to the CEA.[19] To grant an exemption, the CFTC must determine that the exemption is in the public interest, that the exempted transactions will be entered into only by "appropriate persons," and that the exemption will not have a material adverse effect on the ability of the CFTC or a designated contract market to fulfill its duties under the CEA.[20] Further, the FTPA expressly precluded the CFTC from exempting transactions from the Shad-Johnson Accord, including the prohibition of futures contracts on an individual non-exempt security. This limitation, coupled with Congress's

---

the Securities Exchange Act of 1934. 15 U.S.C. §§ 77c, 78c(a)(12). Note, however, that transactions in government securities that are excluded from the CEA by the Treasury Amendment are subject to the provisions of the securities laws enacted in the Government Securities Act, as amended. Government Securities Act of 1986, Pub. L. No. 99-571, 100 Stat. 3208 (codified as amended in scattered sections of 15 U.S.C. and 31 U.S.C.). Although municipal securities are exempt securities under the securities laws, under the Shad-Johnson Accord they are treated like corporate debt and equity securities, foreign sovereign debt securities, and other securities that are not classified as exempt securities under the securities laws. Thus, municipal securities and other securities that are not defined as exempt securities are collectively referred to as "non-exempt securities" in this report.

[18]   Futures Trading Practices Act of 1992, Pub. L. No. 102-546, 106 Stat. 3590.

[19]   H.R. Rep. No. 102-978, 102d Cong, 2d Sess. 83 (1992).

[20]   7 U.S.C. § 6(c). Under the FTPA, "appropriate persons" include banks, insurance companies, investment companies, commodity pools, broker-dealers, FCMs, and governmental entities. A corporation or partnership may be an appropriate person if it has a net worth exceeding $1,000,000 or assets exceeding $5,000,000. The CFTC may determine that the inclusion of other persons is appropriate based on financial or other qualifications or on the application of appropriate regulatory protections.

decision to authorize an exemption (rather than an exclusion) for swap agreements and hybrid instruments, is the origin of concern about the legal status of certain derivatives that reference securities.

Since 1992, the CFTC has used its exemptive authority in connection with each of the three classes of instruments that were specifically discussed in the legislative history of the FTPA: (1) swap agreements;[21] (2) hybrid instruments;[22] and (3) certain OTC energy contracts, including Brent oil contracts, which had been found by one court to be futures contracts.[23] In exercising its authority, the CFTC also reaffirmed the continued applicability of its Policy Statement Concerning Swap Transactions (the "Swap Policy Statement") and Statutory Interpretation Concerning Certain Hybrid Instruments (the "Hybrid Interpretation"), statements of regulatory and enforcement policy with respect to swap agreements and hybrid instruments that had been issued by the CFTC prior to the enactment of the FTPA.[24]

---

[21]   17 C.F.R. pt. 35 (the "Swap Exemption"). Part 35 of the CFTC Regulations exempts swap agreements from most provisions of the CEA, provided that: (a) the swap agreement is entered into solely between eligible swap participants; (b) the swap agreement is not part of a fungible class of agreements that are standardized as to their material economic terms; (c) creditworthiness is a material consideration in entering into the swap agreement; and (d) the swap agreement is not traded on a multilateral transaction execution facility.

[22]   17 C.F.R. pt. 34 (the "Hybrid Instrument Rule").

[23]   Exemption for Certain Contracts Involving Energy Products, 58 Fed. Reg. 21,286 (Apr. 20, 1993). Cf. Transnor (Bermuda) Ltd. v. BP N. Am. Petroleum, 738 F. Supp. 1472 (S.D.N.Y. 1990).

[24]   Policy Statement Concerning Swap Transactions, 54 Fed. Reg. 30,694 (July 21, 1989); Statutory Interpretation Concerning Certain Hybrid Instruments, 55 Fed. Reg. 13,582 (Apr. 11, 1990).

IV. Continuing Legal Uncertainties With Respect to Swap Agreements

A. Background

As a result of limitations in the FTPA and the continuing evolution of the OTC markets, concerns regarding legal uncertainty persist. While the range of OTC derivatives activity currently conducted in the United States generally does not fall within the category of transactions intended to be regulated (or prohibited) as futures or options contracts under the CEA, the Working Group nonetheless recognizes that any reasonable uncertainty can have undesirable effects and should be remedied. Moreover, uncertainty involving OTC derivatives has hampered private sector efforts to utilize electronic trading systems to enhance market efficiency and transparency and clearing facilities to reduce systemic risk in the OTC markets. Accordingly, the Working Group has concluded that a series of amendments to the CEA is necessary.

1. Current Treatment of Swaps under the CEA

In 1989, the CFTC issued the Swap Policy Statement, which reflected the agency's view that "most swap transactions, although possessing elements of futures or options contracts, are not appropriately regulated as such under the [CEA] and regulations."[25] Because the Swap Policy Statement was issued prior to the enactment of the FTPA, the CFTC at the time lacked authority to exempt futures contracts from the provisions of the CEA that require all such contracts to be traded on contract markets approved by the CFTC in order to be legal. Accordingly, some market participants have indicated that they viewed the Swap Policy Statement as an indication that swap agreements covered by the Swap Policy Statement are not futures contracts.

In enacting the FTPA in 1992, Congress indicated that the CFTC should use its authority to exempt swap agreements from the CEA "to the extent that such agreements may be regarded

---

[25]   54 Fed. Reg. at 30,694. The Swap Policy Statement created a non-exclusive safe harbor that the CFTC indicated it would recognize. To qualify for this safe harbor, swap transactions must, among other things, be settled in cash or foreign currency, have "transaction specifications" that are "individually tailored," be "based upon individualized credit determinations," and not be subject to termination by an exchange-style offset mechanism nor "supported by the credit of a clearing organization" or "a mark-to-market margin and variation settlement system designed to eliminate individualized credit risk." Also, to qualify for the non-exclusive safe harbor, swap transactions must be connected to the "parties' line of business" (which may include providing financial intermediation services) and cannot be marketed to the public.

as subject to the provisions of [the CEA]."[26] Thus, while Congress clearly indicated that swap agreements should not be regulated under the CEA, it did not establish whether swaps are commodity futures or options that would be subject to the CEA in the absence of an exemption. In 1993, the CFTC adopted the Swap Exemption,[27] which covers any swap agreement meeting the following criteria:

- The swap agreement must be entered into between eligible swap participants. "Eligible swap participants" are defined to include various regulated financial institutions, business enterprises that meet certain tests relating to total assets or net worth, certain pension funds, state and local governments, and individuals with more than $10 million in total assets.

- The swap agreement may not be part of a fungible class of agreements that are standardized as to their material economic terms.

- The creditworthiness of the parties to the swap agreement must be a material consideration in entering into and determining the terms of the swap agreement.

- The swap agreement may not be entered into and traded on or through a multilateral transaction execution facility (an "MTEF"). The CFTC explained that an MTEF "is a physical or electronic facility in which all market makers and other participants have the ability to execute transactions and bind both parties by accepting offers which are made by one member and open to all members of the facility."[28]

Although the Swap Exemption affords practical relief for a broad range of transactions, concerns about its scope persist. Because Congress never conclusively determined whether swaps would be subject to the CEA in the absence of the exemption, the exact status of these instruments (i.e., whether they are forwards, futures, options, or none of the above) is unclear. Under the Swap Exemption, the CFTC retains anti-fraud and anti-manipulation authority over

---

[26]   7 U.S.C. § 6.

[27]   Exemption for Certain Swap Agreements, 58 Fed. Reg. 5587 (Jan. 22, 1993) (codified at 17 C.F.R. pt. 35).

[28]   Id. at 5591.

otherwise exempted swap agreements, although this retained authority would be available only in instances where a statutory basis for its exercise exists.

Moreover, two actions by the CFTC in 1998 led some market participants to express concerns that the CFTC might modify the Swap Exemption and attempt to impose new regulations on the swap market. First, in a comment letter addressing the SEC's "broker-dealer lite" proposal,[29] the CFTC stated that the SEC's proposal would create the potential for conflict with the CEA to the extent that certain OTC derivative instruments fall within the ambit of the CEA and are subject to the exclusive statutory authority of the CFTC.[30] Participants in the market for swap agreements that reference non-exempt securities, such as equity swaps, credit swaps, and emerging market debt swaps, were particularly concerned by the CFTC's comment letter because statements suggesting that some swap agreements might be viewed as futures contracts were construed to imply questions about the applicability of the Shad-Johnson Accord, which prohibits futures on non-exempt securities (except futures on securities indices on designated contract markets that are cash settled and meet certain other conditions).[31] Subsequently, the CFTC issued a concept release requesting comment on whether regulation of OTC derivatives markets is appropriate and, if so, what form such regulation should take.[32] Some market participants construed the concept release as raising uncertainty about the applicability of the Swap Exemption to certain aspects of the developing OTC markets because it stated that certain OTC derivative products were becoming increasingly standardized, and

---

[29]   OTC Derivatives Dealers, 63 Fed. Reg. 59,362 (Nov. 3, 1998). As adopted by the SEC, this rule provides OTC derivatives dealers affiliated with registered broker-dealers with an alternative regulatory regime in order to facilitate participation by such dealers in the OTC derivatives markets. Under the rule, an OTC dealer is permitted to engage in OTC derivatives transactions that qualify as securities, as well as transactions in non-security OTC derivatives, subject to capital requirements that would be more favorable to such transactions than the traditional broker-dealer regulatory regime.

[30]   Letter from Jean A. Webb, Secretary, CFTC, to Jonathan G. Katz, Secretary, SEC (Feb. 26, 1998).

[31]   The CFTC cannot grant exemptions from the restrictions of the Shad-Johnson Accord. Swap agreements involving non-exempt securities are routinely entered into, however, in reliance on the CFTC's comment in the Swap Policy Statement that most swap transactions are not appropriately regulated as commodity futures or options. Moreover, in adopting the Swap Exemption, the CFTC stated that market participants could continue to rely on the Swap Policy Statement. 58 Fed. Reg. at 5588. In referring to the Swap Policy Statement, the CFTC cited FTPA legislative history stating that Congress did not intend to call into question the legal status of existing securities-linked swaps.

[32]   Over-the-Counter Derivatives, 63 Fed. Reg. 26,114 (May 12, 1998).

because it requested comments on the possibility of developing a regulatory framework under the CEA for electronic trading and clearing of OTC derivatives.

Legislation enacted at the request of Treasury, the Federal Reserve Board, and the SEC in 1998 limited the CFTC's rulemaking authority with respect to swaps and hybrid instruments until March 30, 1999, and froze the pre-existing legal status of swap agreements and hybrid instruments entered into in reliance on the Swap Exemption, the Hybrid Instrument Rule, the Swap Policy Statement, or the Hybrid Interpretation.[33] The legislation reduced legal uncertainty but did not provide a permanent clarification of the legal status of these instruments.

2. Electronic Trading Systems

Technological innovation in the financial markets in recent years has been significant, and it is likely that the pace of change will continue to accelerate in the future. Computer technology has the potential to increase the efficiency, transparency, and liquidity of the financial markets by increasing the speed of transactions and lowering transaction costs. At the same time, new ways of doing business present new questions about the applicability of existing laws.

Both exchange-traded derivatives markets and the OTC markets have begun to make use of new technologies. For example, the Chicago Board of Trade and the Chicago Mercantile Exchange have introduced electronic trading systems that operate in conjunction with the exchanges' traditional floor-trading activities. In the OTC markets, electronic trading systems for foreign currency derivatives have operated for several years, and more recently, an electronic system for interest rate swaps has been developed.

The development of computerized trading systems for OTC derivatives, however, has been affected by uncertainty about the applicability of the CEA. Swap agreements are not currently covered by the Swap Exemption if they are entered into and traded on or through an MTEF. The applicability of the CFTC's definition of MTEF to particular types of systems that may be developed is far from clear, however.

---

[33] Agriculture, Rural Development, Food and Drug Administration, and Related Agencies Appropriations Act, 1999, § 760, as enacted in Omnibus Consolidated and Emergency Supplemental Appropriations Act, 1999, Pub. L. No. 105-277, 112 Stat. 2681, 2681-35 (1998).

Traditionally, participants in the swap market have communicated bid and offer information and entered into swap agreements via telephone and facsimile. Computer technology, however, can allow market participants to communicate with multiple parties at the same time via computer terminals, and to execute transactions automatically. The CFTC has indicated that although electronic communication systems are not MTEFs, systems used to enter orders to execute transactions may be.[34] Market participants, however, have argued that the means used to execute a swap agreement (computer systems rather than telephonic systems) should not alter the regulatory status of the agreement. Market participants have also argued that an electronic system in which the credit policies of each participant are programmed into the system is not an MTEF because an offer made by one participant would only be open to other participants with credit that was deemed acceptable by the offeror. On the other hand, representatives of organized futures exchanges have argued that electronic systems that allow for automated execution operate as exchanges and should be regulated in a similar manner.

3. Clearing Systems

Clearing systems can mitigate the loss that an individual party to a transaction suffers if its counterparty fails to settle an obligation. In a clearing system, obligations of the counterparties may be replaced by obligations of a central counterparty or by obligations of other participants in the system. Often clearing systems also entail a system for sharing losses among surviving participants or for shifting losses to a third party. Thus, clearing systems can serve a valuable function in reducing systemic risk by preventing the failure of a single market participant from having a disproportionate effect on the overall market. Clearing systems also facilitate the offset and netting of obligations arising under contracts that are cleared through the system. Because they may serve to concentrate diffuse credit risks in a single entity, however, clearing systems should be subject to regulatory oversight in order to help ensure that proper risk management procedures are established and implemented and that the clearing system is properly structured.

By its terms, the Swap Exemption "does not extend to transactions that are subject to a clearing system where the credit risk of individual members of the system to each other in a

---

[34]   58 Fed. Reg. at 5591.

transaction to which each is a counterparty is effectively eliminated and replaced by a system of mutualized risk of loss that binds members generally whether or not they are counterparties to the original transaction."[35] The CFTC has indicated, however, that a person seeking to establish a clearing system for swaps might apply for a further exemption from the CEA.[36]

The CFTC's concept release, in which it sought comment on proposed regulatory approaches to clearing systems,[37] as well as questions raised by the CFTC in the context of filings by entities proposing to clear certain products involving government securities,[38] have been construed by some market participants as implicit assertions of CFTC regulatory jurisdiction over OTC derivatives clearing. The Working Group notes that the CEA does not explicitly provide for direct oversight of clearing systems by the CFTC. Rather, CFTC regulation of clearing has developed in connection with the CFTC's oversight of futures exchanges associated with clearing systems. Because the CEA does not specifically provide a framework for the oversight of a clearing system for OTC derivatives, the introduction of clearing systems for OTC financial derivatives raises complex jurisdictional issues that should be resolved. Accordingly, the Working Group has concluded that Congressional action is necessary to establish appropriate policy guidance for the establishment and oversight of clearing systems for OTC derivatives (other than derivatives, such as OTC options on securities, that are themselves securities, for which a clearing regulatory structure already exists under Section 17A of the Securities Exchange Act of 1934).[39]

B.   Recommendations

1.   Enhancing Legal Certainty for Swaps

The members of the Working Group agree that there is no compelling evidence of problems involving bilateral swap agreements that would warrant regulation under the CEA;

---

[35]   Id.

[36]   Id. at 5591 n.30.

[37]   63 Fed. Reg. at 26,122.

[38]   See Securities Exchange Act Release No. 39,623, 63 Fed. Reg. 7022 (Feb. 11, 1998); Securities Exchange Act Release No. 40,623, 63 Fed. Reg. 59,831 (Nov. 5, 1998).

[39]   15 U.S.C. § 78q-1.

accordingly, many types of swap agreements should be excluded from the CEA. The sophisticated counterparties that use OTC derivatives simply do not require the same protections under the CEA as those required by retail investors. In addition, most of the dealers in the swaps market are either affiliated with broker-dealers or FCMs that are regulated by the SEC or the CFTC or are financial institutions that are subject to supervision by bank regulatory agencies. Accordingly, the activities of most derivatives dealers are already subject to direct or indirect federal oversight. To ensure that the unregulated affiliates of broker-dealers and FCMs are subject to appropriate regulatory scrutiny, however, the Working Group reiterates the recommendation made in its report on hedge funds concerning enhanced risk assessments of these affiliates.[40]

Most OTC derivatives are not susceptible to manipulation. The vast majority of the contracts are settled in cash, based on a rate or price determined by a separate highly liquid market with a very large or virtually unlimited deliverable supply. Thus, for example, it is highly unlikely that interest rate swaps could be used to manipulate interest rates. Furthermore, prices established in OTC derivatives transactions do not serve a significant price discovery function.

Due to the characteristics of markets for non-financial commodities with finite supplies, however, the Working Group is unanimously recommending that the exclusion not be extended to agreements involving such commodities. For example, in the case of agricultural commodities, production is seasonal and volatile, and the underlying commodity is perishable, factors that make the markets for these products susceptible to supply and pricing distortions and to manipulation. There have also been several well-known efforts to manipulate the prices of certain metals by attempting to corner the cash or futures markets. Moreover, the cash market for many non-financial commodities is dependent on the futures market for price discovery. The CFTC should, however, retain its current authority to grant exemptions for derivatives involving

---

[40]   President's Working Group on Financial Markets, Hedge Funds, Leverage, and the Lessons of Long-Term Capital Management 38-40 (Apr. 1999). As was the case in the report on hedge funds, Chairman Greenspan of the Federal Reserve declines to endorse the recommendation for expanding risk assessment for the unregulated affiliates of broker-dealers and FCMs, but, in this instance, defers to the judgment of those with supervisory responsibility.

16

non-financial commodities, as it did in 1993 for energy products, where exemptions are in the public interest and otherwise consistent with the CEA.[41]

Accordingly, the Working Group unanimously makes the following recommendations:

- Bilateral swap agreements (including those that reference non-exempt securities) entered into by eligible swap participants, on a principal-to-principal basis, should be excluded from the CEA, provided that the transactions are not conducted on an MTEF (defined in a manner generally consistent with the CFTC's discussion of the term in its adoption of the Swap Exemption). Certain types of electronic trading systems described below should, however, also be excluded from the CEA.

- Because the material economic terms of many swap agreements are similar, the requirement in the current Swap Exemption that swap agreements not be standardized as to their material economic terms should be eliminated. Moreover, as discussed below, the Working Group is recommending that clearing of swap agreements be permitted, subject to appropriate regulatory oversight of the clearing function. Accordingly, insofar as transactions are subject to regulated clearing, the exclusion should not prohibit fungibility of contracts or require that creditworthiness be a material consideration.

- The exclusion should not extend to any swap agreement that involves a non-financial commodity with a finite supply.[42]

- The exclusion should only cover swaps between eligible swaps participants (defined in a manner similar to the definition in the current Swap Exemption). Thus, the exclusion should only be available for regulated financial institutions, business enterprises that meet certain tests relating to total assets or net worth, certain pension funds, state and local governments, and individuals with significant assets. Consideration should be given to further restricting the extent to which individuals qualify for the exclusion by not making it available to natural

---

[41]   In addition, nothing in this report should be construed to affect the scope of exemptions that are currently in effect.

[42]   The CFTC would retain its current exemptive authority for these derivatives.

persons who own and invest on a discretionary basis less than $25 million in investments.

- The CEA should be amended to clarify that a party to a transaction may not avoid performance of its obligations under, or recover losses incurred on, a transaction based solely on the failure of that party (or its counterparty) to comply with the terms of an exclusion or exemption under the CEA.

- To the extent that OTC derivatives transactions between eligible swap participants are excluded from the CEA, they should also be excluded from the coverage of certain state laws (such as laws designed to regulate gambling or bucket shops) that might be construed to prohibit or inappropriately regulate such transactions.

2. Electronic Trading Systems

The Working Group members agree that the introduction of electronic trading systems for OTC derivatives has the potential to promote efficiency and transparency, and, by enhancing liquidity and enabling firms that participate in the systems to impose more reliable internal controls on their traders, to reduce risks. Furthermore, there is not at this time a demonstrable need for regulation of systems with the characteristics described below. The method by which a transaction is executed has no obvious bearing on the need for regulation in markets, such as the markets for financial derivatives, that are not used for price discovery. Moreover, electronic trading systems for OTC derivatives have only just begun to emerge on a widespread basis, and such systems should be allowed to grow, unburdened by a new anticipatory statutory structure that could prove entirely inappropriate to their eventual evolution.

The Working Group has concluded, however, that a broad exclusion from the CEA should be available only for systems in which eligible swap participants trade for their own account. This limitation would provide added assurance of the sophistication of parties eligible to transact on the system (all of whom must, of course, also be eligible swap participants), because systems subject to this limitation would tend to be used only by dealers or regular participants in the market. The absence of agency transactions would also inhibit potential market abuses such as front-running that might otherwise arise.

Accordingly, the Working Group unanimously recommends that Congress amend the CEA to clarify that entering into or trading excluded swap agreements (i.e., agreements between

18

eligible swap participants that do not involve non-financial commodities with finite supplies) through electronic trading systems with certain characteristics does not affect the status of the agreements traded through the system and does not provide a basis for regulation of the system.[43]

- Excluded electronic trading systems should include systems that are clearly not covered by the definition of MTEF in the current Swap Exemption. For example, electronic systems that assist eligible swap participants in communicating about or negotiating a bilateral agreement should be permitted.

- In addition, excluded electronic trading systems should include any form of electronic trading system (including one in which bids and offers are open to all participants), provided that participants in the system must act solely for their own account.

- Exchanges that have been designated as contract markets by the CFTC should be permitted to establish these types of excluded trading systems for qualified swaps.

The Working Group notes that its recommendation to exclude certain trading systems from the CEA should not be viewed as a determination that regulation of these systems may never be appropriate. Limited regulation aimed at enhancing market transparency and price discovery may become necessary under certain circumstances as electronic trading systems for OTC derivatives develop and grow, if problems of the sort that are appropriately addressed by regulation emerge. If so, depending on the specific market, existing regulation, and the problems that regulation would be meant to address, the CFTC's expertise in exchange-traded derivatives could make it an appropriate choice to serve as regulator. At this time, however, it is better to encourage the development of these systems by providing greater legal certainty than to attempt to anticipate an appropriate regulatory scheme for market innovations that are still in the initial stages of development and implementation.

3. Clearing Systems

Clearing of OTC derivatives has the potential to reduce counterparty risks associated with such transactions through risk management techniques that may include mutualizing risks,

---

[43] The CFTC would, however, retain authority to exempt any system that does not qualify for the statutory exclusion.

facilitating offset, and netting. Clearing, however, tends to concentrate risks and certain responsibilities for risk management in a central counterparty or clearinghouse. Consequently, the effectiveness of the clearinghouse's operations and risk management systems is critical for the stability of the markets that it serves. For this reason, the Working Group unanimously recommends that Congress enact legislation to provide a clear basis for the regulation of clearing systems that may develop for OTC derivatives.

In this context, a clearing system would be defined as a system in which the obligations of counterparties to a transaction may be replaced by obligations of a central counterparty or by obligations of other participants in the system, including participants that were not the original counterparties to the transaction. Legislative action would have the beneficial effects of encouraging the development of such systems by clarifying their legal status, subjecting them to appropriate supervision, and ensuring that U.S. firms and markets are not at a competitive disadvantage relative to their foreign counterparties.

The Working Group believes that a comprehensive regulatory framework should contain provisions:

- to authorize clearing organizations that clear futures, commodity options, and options on futures also to clear OTC derivatives (other than OTC derivatives that are securities, such as securities options), subject to the oversight of the CFTC;

- to authorize securities clearing agencies (which are subject to the oversight of the SEC) also to clear OTC derivatives (other than instruments involving a non-financial commodity with a finite supply);

- to authorize the CFTC to develop rules for the establishment and regulation of clearing systems for OTC derivatives involving a non-financial commodity with a finite supply (to the extent that they are exempted by the CFTC in a manner that allows clearing);

- to require all other clearing systems for OTC derivatives to organize as a bank, bank subsidiary or affiliate, or Edge Act corporation that would be subject to the supervisory jurisdiction of the Federal Reserve or the Office of the Comptroller of the Currency;

20

- to establish that a clearing system subject to regulation by one agency would not become subject to regulation by another agency as a result of clearing OTC derivatives;

- to establish explicitly that clearing systems are not, and do not by themselves imply the presence of, MTEFs, and that an electronic trading system that is excluded from the CEA does not become subject to the CEA because transactions entered into through the trading system are also cleared; and

- to allow clearing through foreign clearing systems that are supervised by a foreign financial regulator that the appropriate U.S. regulator has determined satisfies appropriate standards.

4. Exchange-Traded Derivatives Markets

The Working Group's recommendations with respect to electronic trading and clearing for OTC derivatives and the recommended clarification of the Treasury Amendment discussed below are intended to remove legal obstacles to innovations that have the potential to increase efficiency, transparency, liquidity, and competition and to reduce systemic risk. Some market participants have argued, however, that U.S. futures exchanges are at a competitive disadvantage to OTC derivatives markets as the result of CEA regulation, and that the introduction of electronic trading and clearing for derivatives outside of the CEA has the potential to exacerbate the perceived imbalance.

The Working Group acknowledges that the enactment of its proposal for a swap exclusion that does not bar agreements that are fungible and standardized — a necessary corollary of permitting efficient electronic execution and clearing — would blur some of the distinctions between futures and swaps. Therefore, the recommended exclusion would create differences in the level of regulation between OTC derivatives that are electronically traded and cleared and products offered by futures exchanges that may have some similar characteristics. The difference would be mitigated to some extent if the Working Group's recommendations are adopted, because futures exchanges could establish electronic trading systems and clearing systems under the same conditions as their competitors. Floor-traded futures contracts with some economic characteristics similar to the derivatives for which electronic trading systems might develop would, however, face different levels or different forms of regulation.

Where regulation exists, it should serve valid public policy goals. The justifications generally cited for regulation of the futures markets include the goals of protecting retail customers from unfair practices, protecting the price discovery function, and guarding against manipulation. With similar policy goals in mind, the Working Group has recommended limiting the proposed exclusion for swap agreements to eligible swap participants trading for their own account, and, as discussed below, is also recommending that the CFTC be provided with clear authority to regulate transactions in foreign currency between retail customers and entities other than banks, broker-dealers, and their affiliates.[44] It has also recommended limiting proposed exclusions to markets that are not readily susceptible to manipulation and that do not currently serve a significant price discovery function.

To the extent that particular exchange-traded futures markets are accessible to retail customers, serve a price discovery function, or may be susceptible to manipulation, some regulation of these markets may be warranted. To the extent that these factors are less relevant to certain futures markets, regulatory adjustments may be necessary. Accordingly, existing regulatory structures (particularly those applicable to markets for financial futures) should be reviewed to determine whether they are appropriately tailored to serve valid regulatory goals. Exchange trading should not be subject to regulations that do not have a public policy justification. Although specific recommendations about the regulatory structure applicable to exchange-traded futures are beyond the scope of this report, the CFTC is currently examining the CEA to determine the extent to which modifications of the status quo are necessary.

Although the CEA gives the CFTC broad authority to grant exemptive relief if it determines it is in the public interest, the CFTC notes that the Conference Report for the FTPA specifically stated that "[t]he goal of providing the Commission with broad exemptive authority is not to prompt a wide-scale deregulation of markets falling within the ambit of the [CEA]."[45] Accordingly, the CFTC believes that further Congressional direction is necessary. In deference to the CFTC's views, the Working Group as a whole believes that the enactment of its recommendations with respect to OTC derivatives should be accompanied by explicit authority

---

[44] Transactions in government securities that are excluded from the CEA by the Treasury Amendment are already subject to regulation under the Government Securities Act.

[45] H.R. Rep. 102-978, 102d Cong., 2d Sess. 81 (1992).

for the CFTC to provide appropriate regulatory relief for exchange-traded financial futures if deemed by the CFTC to be consistent with the public interest.[46]

---

[46]   Such authority should not, however, permit the CFTC to provide exemptive or other regulatory relief from the requirements of the Shad-Johnson Accord. See supra note 16 and accompanying text and infra part VIII.A.

V.   The Treasury Amendment

A.   Background

Treasury proposed the Treasury Amendment in 1974 because of a concern that the very broad definition of the term "commodity" in the Commodity Futures Trading Commission Act would subject the OTC markets for government securities and foreign currency to regulation under the CEA. In the absence of the Treasury Amendment (or another applicable exemption or exclusion), any futures contract involving foreign currency or government securities would be illegal unless traded on a contract market approved by the CFTC.

There are several rationales for this exclusion from the CEA. These markets serve important macroeconomic functions that are best served by minimal regulation. The main participants in the foreign currency markets are largely sophisticated institutions, such as commercial and investment banks, central banks, foreign exchange dealers, corporations, and pension and mutual funds, that are well-informed and do not need protection. The market is highly efficient and has served the needs of the international business community well. Similarly, the government securities market is one of the most efficient markets in the world and has served the Treasury and the taxpayers well. Moreover, since 1986, government securities have been regulated under the Government Securities Act, and government securities transactions are subject to the anti-fraud and anti-manipulation provisions of the federal securities laws.

Unfortunately, the language of the Treasury Amendment, while helpful, has continued to provoke debate and litigation concerning the breadth of the exclusion it provides from the CEA. Prior to 1997, there was a disagreement as to whether foreign currency options were "transactions in" foreign currency that were excluded from the CEA. In 1997, the Supreme Court clarified that the phrase "transactions in" as used in the Treasury Amendment includes options.[47]

There has also been legal uncertainty associated with the so-called "unless" clause of the Treasury Amendment, which provides that the CEA exclusion for transactions in government securities, foreign currency, and the other listed instruments is available "unless such transactions involve the sale thereof for future delivery conducted on a board of trade." The

---

[47]   Dunn v. CFTC, 519 U.S. 465 (1997).

24

CEA broadly defines "board of trade" to mean "any exchange or association of persons who are engaged in the business of buying or selling any commodity."[48] Treasury has argued that an overly expansive application of this definition would nullify the Treasury Amendment. Because a court will generally not interpret a statutory provision in a manner that renders it meaningless, Treasury has argued that the term, as used in the Treasury Amendment, should be viewed solely as a means of preserving the CFTC's authority to regulate transactions that occur on organized futures exchanges.

The CFTC, however, has expressed concerns that the Treasury Amendment may be construed to limit its authority to take enforcement action against bucket shops that enter into fraudulent foreign currency transactions with members of the general public. In several enforcement actions it has taken the position that the Treasury Amendment should be interpreted in light of its legislative history, which focused on the need to shelter institutional OTC markets from regulation under the CEA. Thus, the CFTC has held that an "association of persons" entering into transactions with the general public is a board of trade.[49]

The case law on the subject is inconclusive. The only Court of Appeals that has addressed this question reached a decision that is generally consistent with Treasury's interpretation.[50] Similarly, one judge of the District Court for the Southern District of New York has interpreted "board of trade" to mean "organized futures exchange" in a case involving transactions between a wealthy individual and an investment bank, but another judge on the same court has adopted a more expansive interpretation of the term board of trade in a case involving a retail bucket shop.[51]

From a policy perspective, these conflicting interpretations of the Treasury Amendment create a "Catch-22" situation. On the one hand, because the text of the Treasury Amendment makes no specific reference to the institutional market, there is a risk that a broad interpretation of "board of trade" in a case involving a bucket shop could later be applied to invalidate

---

[48]   7 U.S.C. § 1a.

[49]   See, e.g., In re: Global Link Miami Corp., CFTC Docket No. 98-1 (May 24, 1999).

[50]   CFTC v. Frankwell Bullion Ltd., 99 F.3d 299 (9th Cir. 1996).

[51]   Compare Kwiatkowski v. Bear Stearns Co., 1997 U.S. Dist. LEXIS 13,078 (Aug. 28, 1997) with Rosner v. Korbean International Investment Corp., 1998 U.S. Dist. LEXIS 7353 (May 18, 1998).

legitimate transactions in the institutional OTC market. On the other hand, construing the term to preserve only the CFTC's authority over organized futures exchanges that trade instruments covered by the Treasury Amendment impairs the CFTC's ability to take enforcement action in cases involving retail fraud.

Uncertainty has also been expressed with respect to screen-based electronic trading systems and clearing systems for Treasury Amendment instruments. Market participants have expressed the concern that the development of such entities may be hampered by the possibility that they would be considered "boards of trade."

B.   Recommendations

The Working Group members unanimously recommend that the Treasury Amendment be clarified by replacing the term "board of trade" in the Treasury Amendment with the term "organized exchange." The definition of the new term would preserve the CFTC's authority to regulate transactions in Treasury Amendment instruments[52] to the extent that such transactions occur on an exchange that is open to retail or agency transactions and that serves a self-regulatory function with respect to its members or participants (or enters into arrangements with another entity to serve such a function on its behalf). Except as discussed below with respect to certain retail foreign currency transactions, however, the provision would exclude the rest of the markets for Treasury Amendment instruments from the CEA. Accordingly, the scope of electronic trading permitted outside of the CEA would be broader for Treasury Amendment instruments than for other financial instruments.[53] As would be the case for excluded swaps, regulated clearing of Treasury Amendment products would be allowed without affecting the exclusion from the CEA.

To address the problems associated with foreign currency bucket shops, however, the Working Group also unanimously recommends that the CEA be amended to provide that transactions in foreign currency futures and options are subject to the CEA if they are entered

---

[52]   Treasury Amendment instruments that are securities or options on foreign currency that trade on a securities exchange would continue to be subject to the jurisdiction of the SEC.

[53]   Thus, for example, an electronic trading system for Treasury Amendment products that allows the execution of transactions through agents would be excluded from the CEA as long as it did not also serve (or arrange for another entity to serve) a self-regulatory function. It should be noted, however, that transactions in government securities occurring outside of the CEA are subject to the Government Securities Act.

into between a retail customer and an entity that is neither regulated or supervised by the SEC or a federal banking regulator nor affiliated with such a regulated or supervised entity. [54]

---

[54]   As discussed <u>supra</u> at note 40 and accompanying text, the Working Group is recommending enhanced oversight of the currently unregulated affiliates of broker-dealers.

VI. Hybrid Instruments

A. Background

The CFTC's Hybrid Instrument Rule exempts securities and bank deposits that have some of the characteristics of commodity futures or options from all of the provisions of the CEA except the Shad-Johnson Accord.[55] Under the exemption, the value of that portion of a hybrid instrument that derives its value from aspects of the instrument that are not related to the value of commodities must be equal to or greater than the value (as determined by a calculation methodology specified in the exemption) of the aspects that are commodity-related. In addition, the hybrid instrument must be subject to securities or banking laws and sold to persons eligible to purchase the instrument under such laws, and must satisfy certain criteria regarding marketing, payment terms, and settlement. In adopting the Hybrid Instrument Rule, the CFTC did not assert that it retained anti-fraud or anti-manipulation jurisdiction over instruments that are within the scope of the exemption.

Market participants have generally been satisfied that the exemption provides a sufficient measure of legal certainty to the markets for the covered instruments. As in the case of swaps, however, there is legal uncertainty associated with hybrid instruments that reference non-exempt securities. If a court determined that such instruments were subject to the Shad-Johnson Accord's prohibition on single-stock futures, the Hybrid Instrument Rule would not apply to them, because the CFTC lacks authority to provide an exemption from the provisions of the Shad-Johnson Accord.[56]

Last year, the CFTC's concept release sought comment on whether the Hybrid Instrument Rule should be amended to expand the CFTC's jurisdiction over exempted instruments. Since hybrid instruments are securities or bank products, this raised questions about whether a broader assertion of authority by the CFTC would lead to jurisdictional disputes and increased legal uncertainty. If a hybrid instrument were legally determined to be a futures contract or a commodity option, the exclusive jurisdiction clause could imply that only the CFTC could regulate the instrument, even if it is a security or a bank product. Conversely, if an

---

[55]   17 C.F.R. pt. 34.

[56]   The Hybrid Instrument Rule has also been criticized by some because of its complexity.

instrument is not a futures contract or a commodity option, an assertion of jurisdiction by the CFTC could lack a legal foundation.

B.   Recommendations

Hybrid instruments are either securities or bank products, and are regulated as such. Nevertheless, there is not general agreement that all hybrid instruments should be entirely excluded from the CEA. Moreover, the Working Group does not believe that codification of the Hybrid Instrument Rule is necessary to enhance legal certainty. To enhance legal certainty for hybrid instruments that reference non-exempt securities, however, the Working Group unanimously recommends enactment of a provision to clarify that the Shad-Johnson Accord shall not be construed to apply to hybrid instruments that have been exempted from the CEA. In addition, as discussed below, a modification of the CEA's exclusive jurisdiction clause is necessary to ensure that questions do not arise as to the authority of the SEC and bank regulatory agencies with respect to hybrid instruments.

The CFTC believes that it may be possible to develop a new rule that provides greater legal certainty and addresses certain of the perceived weaknesses in the current rule but does not exclude all hybrid instruments from the CEA. In recognition of the interests of the SEC and the bank regulatory agencies in this area, however, the CFTC will not propose any new rule relating to hybrid instruments without the concurrence of the other members of the Working Group. The other Working Group members will work with the CFTC on developing the rule and will give serious consideration to any proposals that it may make.

VII. Exclusive Jurisdiction

A. Background

The CEA confers on the CFTC "exclusive jurisdiction" over commodity futures and options thereon, which means that these instruments cannot be regulated by any other federal or state agency (except in certain limited circumstances where the CEA explicitly contemplates shared authority between the CFTC and another agency). This provision of the CEA has generated legal uncertainty concerning the appropriate regulator and scheme of regulation for complex derivative instruments that possess attributes of securities and futures contracts. For example, in Chicago Mercantile Exchange v. SEC[57] the Seventh Circuit Court of Appeals held that "index participations," a type of instrument based on the value of a basket of securities, were both securities and futures contracts, but that the CFTC's exclusive jurisdiction over futures contracts precluded SEC action with respect to such instruments.[58]

B. Recommendations

The Working Group members agree that the exclusive jurisdiction clause of the CEA should be modified. Treasury, the Federal Reserve, and the SEC believe that the exclusive jurisdiction clause should apply only to transactions in futures contracts or options on futures contracts effected on designated contract markets, and that the clause should be clarified by providing that the CFTC's jurisdiction over such transactions is not exclusive in instances where the CEA or some other federal statute specifically grants another agency authority. At this time, the CFTC believes that it has not had sufficient opportunity to evaluate all of the possible ramifications of this proposal. The CFTC would, however, support an amendment to the CEA to provide that insofar as hybrid instruments may be subject to the CEA, the exclusive jurisdiction clause shall not be construed to limit the authority of the SEC and the bank regulatory agencies

---

[57]   883 F.2d 537 (7th Cir. 1989), cert. denied sub nom. Investment Co. Inst. v. SEC, 496 U.S. 936 (1990).

[58]   In two recent enforcement cases, the SEC has been challenged by defendants on jurisdictional grounds, and asked to brief the court on why the exclusive jurisdiction clause does not preclude the SEC from bringing an enforcement action in a case involving instruments that would purportedly be subject to the CEA in the absence of the Treasury Amendment. See SEC v. Bankers Alliance Corp., Civ. No. 95-0428 (PLF) (D.D.C.); SEC v. Unique Financial Concepts, Inc., No. 99-4033 (11th Cir.).

with respect to such instruments. Accordingly, the Working Group unanimously recommends that Congress adopt this clarification of the exclusive jurisdiction clause. In addition, the CFTC agrees that it will continue to work with the other Working Group agencies to develop its views on the merits of a broader modification of the exclusive jurisdiction clause.

VIII. Other Issues

A.   Single-Stock Futures

The Working Group members agree that the current prohibition on single-stock futures can be repealed if issues about the integrity of the underlying securities market and regulatory arbitrage are resolved. Because a single-stock future is a contract to purchase or sell a security and functions as a very close substitute for the underlying security, it may be appropriate to regulate these instruments as securities. On the other hand, because it is likely that such instruments would trade on organized futures exchanges, it may also be necessary to tailor legislation and regulation so as to take account of institutional differences between the futures markets and the securities markets.

From the perspective of the securities laws, the issues raised by trading of single-stock futures include levels of margin, insider trading, sales practices, real-time trade reporting, and activities of floor brokers, as well as the exclusive jurisdiction of the CFTC over futures contract markets. From the perspective of the commodity futures laws, the issues raised by these instruments include clearing, segregation, large trader reporting, and direct surveillance.[59]

The SEC is the agency with expertise concerning regulation of securities and stock exchanges; the CFTC is the agency with expertise concerning the regulation of futures markets. Thus, the Working Group unanimously recommends that these agencies work together and with Congress to determine whether the trading of single-stock futures should be permitted and if so, under what conditions.

The Working Group also notes that the futures exchanges' ability to offer a greater variety of equity-related products has been advanced by a recent court decision that interprets the SEC's authority to review proposed securities index futures contracts under the Shad-Johnson Accord[60] and by the lack of SEC objection to a recent single-sector futures contract on the Internet Stock Price Index.[61]

---

[59]   Treasury notes that questions as to the appropriate tax treatment of such instruments would also have to be addressed.

[60]   Board of Trade of the City of Chicago v. SEC, 1999 U.S. App. LEXIS 18469 (7th Cir. 1999).

[61]   See Letter from Robert L.D. Colby, Deputy Director, Division of Market Regulation, SEC, to Steven Manaster, Director, Division of Economic Analysis, CFTC (Mar. 12, 1999).

B.   Regulatory and Tax Arbitrage

A criticism of OTC derivatives is that they can be used as a means to circumvent regulation. For example, institutional investors may be prohibited from investing in certain types of financial instruments but may be able to assume a nearly identical economic position by entering into a derivatives transaction. The Working Group is aware that the derivatives industry has been quite creative in tailoring particular products to achieve certain regulatory results that were not originally intended. As difficult as the task may be, the Working Group nonetheless believes that in most instances such "regulatory arbitrage" issues should be addressed by amending the underlying statutes and regulations that most closely pertain to the regulatory goal to be achieved, and should not be used as a basis for the imposition of an unwarranted regulatory regime on derivatives. For example, judgments about the authority of pension funds or state and local governments to enter into certain derivatives transactions should be made through the laws that directly govern such entities.

Derivatives can also be used to achieve certain tax results that differ from those resulting from investments in the underlying commodity or instrument. For example, derivatives have been used in ways that arguably change the character, source, or timing of income. Treasury is particularly concerned about these issues and has been addressing them through changes in regulation and by proposing legislative changes. For example, the assumption of a derivatives position that eliminates substantially all of the economic risk of an investment asset held by the taxpayer is now viewed as a constructive sale and is thus a taxable event. Again, as in the area of regulation, the creativity of the derivatives industry in this area has given rise to many issues of concern to Treasury and the Internal Revenue Service. Tax creativity in the structuring of transactions, however, is not new, and the Working Group believes that these issues need to be addressed under the Internal Revenue Code and regulations.

C.   Netting

The Working Group reiterates its strong support for the improvements in the close-out netting regime for derivatives and other financial instruments under the Bankruptcy Code and bank insolvency law recommended in its April 1999 report, Hedge funds, Leverage, and the Lessons of Long-Term Capital Management. As discussed in that report, there are improvements currently under consideration by Congress that would, if adopted, reduce systemic risk. Specifically, these proposals would improve the netting regime under the Bankruptcy Code by expanding and clarifying definitions of the financial contracts eligible for netting and by explicitly allowing eligible counterparties to net across different types of contracts, such as swaps, security contracts, repurchase agreements, and forward contracts. They would also clarify bankruptcy procedures for an entity organized in a foreign jurisdiction that has its principal business in the United States and would help to ensure that in a U.S. ancillary proceeding there would not be an issuance of a judicial stay preventing an eligible counterparty from exercising contractual termination, netting, and liquidation rights recognized under U.S. law. Finally, the netting provisions would clarify the netting regime for certain financial contracts in the case of a bank failure. The Working Group believes that these proposals should be enacted into law.

D.   Derivatives Dealers

Derivatives dealers are entities whose business consists primarily of entering into derivative contracts with end users and other dealers. Derivatives dealers may also use OTC derivative instruments to hedge their own financial risks, including risks incurred to obtain desirable financing terms, and to speculate on market movements. Most OTC derivatives dealers in the U.S. are banks or affiliates of banks, or affiliates of broker-dealers or FCMs. Banks and their affiliates are subject to consolidated supervision by banking regulators, but the affiliates of broker-dealers and FCMs are generally unregulated, although the SEC and the CFTC have limited authority to obtain information about the activities of such affiliates, and the SEC has instituted a special regulatory scheme for derivatives dealers that conduct a limited securities business. A small number of U.S. derivatives dealers are affiliated with entities that are not subject to banking or securities regulation, such as insurance companies, finance companies, and energy companies.

With respect to OTC derivatives dealers, private counterparty discipline currently is the primary mechanism relied upon for achieving the public policy objective of reducing systemic risk. Government regulation should serve to supplement, rather than substitute for, private market discipline. In general, private counterparty credit risk management has been employed effectively by both regulated and unregulated dealers of OTC derivatives, and the tools required by federal regulators already exist. In its report on <u>Hedge Funds, Leverage, and the Lessons of</u>

Long-Term Capital Management, however, the Working Group concluded that limitations on the access of the SEC, the CFTC, and Treasury to information about the activities of the unregulated affiliates of broker-dealers and FCMs constituted a gap in the system of financial market oversight that should be filled by providing the relevant agencies with enhanced authority to obtain additional risk assessment information. Because of the importance of these affiliates in the OTC derivatives market, the Working Group reiterates this recommendation.[62]

By contrast, the activities of derivatives dealers that are not affiliated with banks, broker-dealers, or FCMs constitute a small share of the overall market, although the extent of their participation in certain markets, such as the market for energy derivatives, is quite significant.[63] In light of their small market share and the apparent effectiveness of private counterparty discipline in constraining the risk-taking of such derivatives dealers, the Working Group is not recommending legislative action with respect to such derivatives dealers at this time, but believes that continued monitoring of their activity is appropriate.

---

[62] But see supra note 40.

[63] Unaffiliated OTC derivatives dealers are active primarily in the markets for derivatives on non-financial commodities, which account for only a fraction of a percent of derivatives activity. See supra note 7 and accompanying text. Moreover, in 1998, the top 25 derivatives dealers worldwide were banks, securities firms, or affiliates thereof. Swaps Monitor, vol. 12, no. 19 (Aug. 2, 1999).